EQUIPMENT & MATERIALS

LOOKING AFTER BRUSHES

1 *Always have on hand a jar of clean tap water in which to rinse out your brushes while painting. Avoid doing this to stencil brushes, as a wet brush will cause the paint to seep under the stencil.*
2 *Never leave a brush standing in water, or the bristles will splay and bend.*
3 *When you have finished painting for the day, rinse the brushes gently in some clean water. Try to remove any dried paint without separating the bristles too much.*
4 *While the brush is wet, use your fingers to wipe gently along the shaft and over the bristles to keep them pointed.*
5 *To clean a brush that has been used with oil-based paints, rinse it out in turpentine or white spirit, then wash in warm, soapy water and leave to dry.*
6 *Store brushes upright in a jam jar or lying flat on a clean paper towel.*

THIS CHAPTER DESCRIBES the basic equipment, paints and other materials you will need in order to carry out the projects in this book. Wherever possible I have suggested items that are easily available. In my early days as a decorative painter I was often frustrated and thwarted by the lack of suitable paints and products, but now, thankfully, it is possible to find a much wider range.

BRUSHES

You don't need to buy a large selection of brushes to do decorative painting, but they do have to be of reasonable quality, otherwise you will be forever picking loose bristles out of your finished paintwork.

Brushes for base coats

Flat brushes are used for applying base coats. The size you need depends on what you are painting, but I find that a 2.5cm (1in) brush is a versatile size, while 2cm (¾in) is good for fairly small items. For larger surfaces, a 5cm (2in) or 7.5cm (3in) decorator's brush is useful.

Stencil brushes

Stencilling is sometimes done with flat brushes or sponges, but for the projects in this book stencil brushes are best. These round brushes have short bristles that are cut to give a flat edge. Stencil brushes come in different sizes, but No. 8 brushes will be suitable for the projects in this book. You'll need a few, so you can use similar colours on each and not have to keep dipping the brush into water to clean it.

Brushes for decorative painting

Round artist's brushes are used for decorative painting. Sable is the most expensive but there are some very good-quality synthetic-and-sable brushes. You will need the following sizes:
No. 1 for outlining and detailing on smaller motifs
No. 4 for outlining and detailing on larger motifs, and for filling in, shading and highlighting smaller motifs
No. 6 for filling in, shading and highlighting larger motifs
No. 8 for filling in large surface areas.

Varnishing and antiquing brushes

Flat brushes are used for varnishing as well as for base coats, but you should not use them interchangeably. A 2.5cm (1in) brush is a good size for the projects in this book.

This type of brush is also used to apply antiquing liquid. Because it has to be small enough to work the liquid into corners and intricate detailing, I recommend that you use a 2cm (¾in) brush.

PAINTS FOR DECORATIVE WORK

For the past few years I have used emulsion paints for decorative work (both hand-painting and stencilling). I simply choose colours from a colour chart, have a tin of each mixed at the shop, and then, at home, pour the amounts of paint I need for a project into screw-top jars. A 750ml (1¼pt) or 1L (1¾pt) tin will last a long time if you look after it, but if you don't need that much, 250ml (8fl oz) sample pots are a good size. Alternatively, you could use craft paint, several brands of which are now available. Usually marketed as stencil paints, they are generally of good quality and come in a wide range of tempting colours, although you don't get a lot of paint for your money. I use gold paint a lot. Although oil-based gold takes a few hours to dry and can lift if you are not careful when varnishing it, I prefer it because it looks richer than acrylic. Nevertheless, acrylic golds can be very effective, are quick-drying and can be cleaned easily in water. In most cases you should varnish oil-based gold with oil-based varnish, and acrylic gold with acrylic varnish.

BASE COATS

Choosing a base colour can be difficult. The colours I have chosen are a guide – it is up to you, the artist, to put your individual imprint on something by choosing a base colour personal to you.

The type of surface you are working on will dictate whether you need to use water-based or oil-based paint for the base coat.

Water-based paint

Emulsion (both vinyl matt and vinyl silk), acrylic and acrylic-eggshell paints are all water-based. They are fairly fast-drying with relatively low odour, and you can wash your brush in water after use. They are particularly suitable for the following surfaces:

Walls Bare or painted plaster, or walls covered with lining paper, can be painted.

Untreated white wood This wood has not been stained, painted, lacquered or waxed.

MDF Medium-density fibreboard, or MDF, takes water-based paints beautifully. It is quite absorbent so you will need to apply a second coat to give some depth and texture.

Terracotta This is very porous and can sometimes be a little rough but it takes water-based paints extremely well.

Fabric If you are painting something that will require washing, do a test swatch first and then wash it to make sure it is colourfast. Use a craft paint for fabrics and follow the instructions on the product label.

Oil-based paint

This is suitable for all surfaces except fabric. It comes in various formulae and finishes: gloss, satin, mid-sheen, eggshell, matt and undercoat. I *never* use gloss paint, as the water-based decorative paints that I use will not adhere to the very shiny surface. Therefore, for an oil-based background, use a mid-sheen, satin or eggshell finish, as these are all suitable for stencilling, drawing chalk or pencil lines, and eventually painting with water-based decorative paints. People have often challenged me on this, saying that it is

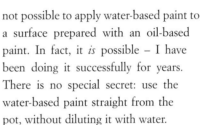

not possible to apply water-based paint to a surface prepared with an oil-based paint. In fact, it *is* possible – I have been doing it successfully for years. There is no special secret: use the water-based paint straight from the pot, without diluting it with water.

DRAWING MATERIALS

Pencils are used for lightly drawing the design on the surface, whether freehand or using templates, and for adding detail to stencilled shapes prior to painting. Choose a medium (HB) lead, and keep an eraser and ruler at hand.

Chalk is excellent for drawing onto large or awkwardly-shaped surfaces, oil-based paint or dark colours. It can be wiped off with a damp cloth.

PAINT SUITABILITY

Surface	Water-based paint	Oil-based paint
Walls	✔	✔
Untreated white wood	✔	✔
Varnished or painted wood		✔
MDF	✔	✔
Laminate		✔
Fabric	✔	
Tin and other metals		✔
Terracotta	✔	✔
Ceramic		✔
Enamel		✔

BUILDING UP
A DESIGN

ONCE YOU HAVE CHOSEN your colours, prepared the surface of your project and painted the base colour, if any, you are ready to paint the design. Don't be intimidated by the prospect – if you carefully follow the steps for each project, you will be amazed at what you can achieve.

To complement the step-by-step photographs, I have prepared hand-painted artwork for many of the projects so you can see the designs – and in particular, the brushwork – in much greater detail. These artworks, which are all of generous size, can also be traced directly from the book onto clear acetate or tracing paper for use as stencils or templates. For the projects that don't have these artworks, trace-off motifs are supplied at the back of the book.

Every project involves drawing or stencilling a design, filling in the shapes with paint, then adding detail, shadows and high-lights. The photographic steps for each project show the design building up through these stages, while large artworks show some projects in greater detail.

FILLING IN
THE BASIC SHAPES

Depending on the project and your own preferences, the design is transferred to the surface by drawing it on freehand, by drawing around a template (see pages 18–19) or by stencilling the basic shapes (again, see pages 18–19). Whichever method is used, the next stage generally involves filling in the shapes with colour. If they have already been sten-cilled, the purpose of filling in is simply to make the stencilled areas more opaque.

Use whichever brush is recommended in the project – the size you will need depends on the size of the shapes you are filling in. Large shapes may require a second coat of paint after the first has dried, particularly if the paint is not very opaque.

DRAWING
THE DETAILS

Once the shapes are filled in, the details can be added using pencil or chalk. This is often the most daunting stage of building up a design. It took me some time to gain confidence when doing animals' legs, beaks and features, and I am still not confident about drawing human figures! Learn to make the most of the images you are good at and keep practising the others. Remember, it doesn't matter if you don't get it right the first, second or even twentieth time – it *is* naive art, after all, so don't be too self-critical.

Using pencil or chalk, lightly draw in any components that were not included on the stencil or template. Have an eraser ready, but before you condemn something to being rubbed out, first decide what is wrong with it. That way, you will be able to move in the right direction at the next attempt.

PAINTING
THE DETAILS

When you are satisfied with the pencil or chalk lines, paint them in the appropriate colours. This stage should be fairly straight-forward, as you will already have drawn the detail – you just need to follow those lines. You will probably find that you gain confidence quickly.

Use the brushes specified in the project to paint the details – I generally recommend a No. 1 or No. 4 artist's brush for this stage. Again, some may require a second coat of paint after the first has dried.

Sometimes it is a good idea to water down the paint a little to help it flow off the brush. This makes painting repetitive patterns much easier, whether it is the detail on a cockerel's wing or an intricate pattern.

The final stage is to make the design look more realistic by shading and highlighting it. This is covered in detail overleaf. Once this is complete and the paint is dry, erase any visible pencil lines, and then varnish the object if desired.

SHADING & HIGHLIGHTING

THIS IS ONE OF THE KEY techniques in my work, setting it apart from similar styles. Although it is a simple procedure, it transforms a flat painted design into a livelier, more realistic effect. Shading and highlighting a painted motif makes it look three-dimensional, as though light is shining on it, creating shadows in some places and highlights in others.

In real life, shadows form in areas that light does not reach (such as crevices and the underside of an object), while highlights occur on the uppermost or outermost part of the surface. The technique of shading and highlighting with paint tries to imitate this. In very realistic painting, artists decide beforehand where the light shining on the design is coming from, and then make all the shadows and highlights consistent with this. However, for my work I don't attempt to achieve that degree of realism. More often than not, it bears no relation to how natural light would fall on an object – but it does stop the motif from looking flat and uninteresting.

For the projects in this book, shading and highlighting are generally done after the colours have been filled in and the details added. Here are some simple guidelines for undertaking it successfully.

ADDING
SHADOWS
AND
HIGHLIGHTS

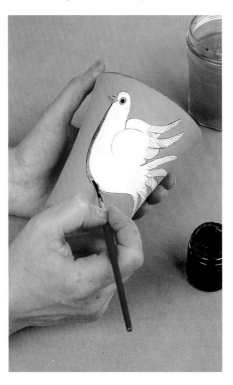

1 Apply slightly watered-down black paint along the underside of the design using a No. 4 artist's brush (or a size specified in the project). Work on only a small area at a time.

2 Quickly but carefully smudge the wet paint with your fingertip, blending into the motif rather than out of it. (In the example shown here, keep the black shading on the white bird, not on the blue area.)

SHADING

Add a drop of water to some black paint, to stop it from looking too dense and heavy. Dip a No. 4 artist's brush (or a size specified in the project) into the black, and carefully paint a line just inside the motif. Start shading on the underside, as this is the area most likely to be in shadow. Don't attempt to shade more than 2–3cm (about 1in) at a time, as the paint will dry quite quickly.

To soften the line, use your fingertip to smudge the paint and blend it in towards the centre of the motif. If it looks too dark, water it down a little more. If, on the other hand, you can hardly see it, add a little more black. It is better to build up the effect gradually than to overdo it.

When you become familiar with this technique, you will begin to recognize which areas can be shaded to greatest effect. Look through the artwork pages of this book to see which portions I have shaded. It's also useful to examine objects in real life to see where the shadows occur.

HIGHLIGHTING

Highlights do not have to be quite so precise. A dab or streak of white – applied with the brush and smudged with your finger – on the upper part of a motif creates a lovely contrast with the shaded area at the bottom. Highlights are also applied to the eyes of animals, as little white dots in the centres; these are not smudged.

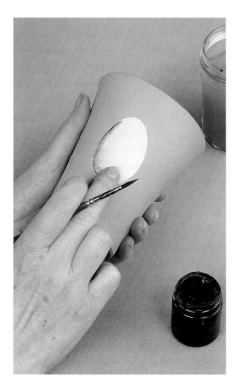

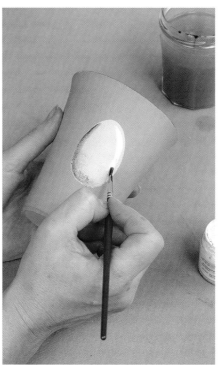

3 An egg, painted here on the other side of the pot, is an excellent motif on which to practise shading.

4 To highlight the egg, add a stroke of white on the top part, and on the opposite side to the shading, using a No. 4 artist's brush. Smudge it towards the middle of the egg using your clean finger.

USING STENCILS & TEMPLATES

YOU CAN USE the artworks that appear with some of the projects, and also the motifs at the back of the book, to make your own stencils and templates. Stencils and templates are opposites: if you cut out an image from paper, the cut-out piece would be the template, and the remaining piece with the hole would be the stencil.

Some projects lend themselves to using stencils, others to templates, and still others to a combination of the two. I use stencilling as a quick way of applying colour, which I then paint over by hand. At other times, all the colour needs to be painted in by hand, so I simply draw in the shape first, either freehand or using a template.

YOU WILL NEED

For stencils
- ✪ *Acetate*
- ✪ *Trace-off motif or your own drawing*
- ✪ *Fine-nibbed permanent marker*
- ✪ *Cutting mat or thick cardboard*
- ✪ *Sharp scalpel or craft knife*
- ✪ *Repositionable spray glue*
- ✪ *Masking tape (optional)*
- ✪ *Water-based paint*
- ✪ *Stencil brush*
- ✪ *Artist's brush*

For templates
- ✪ *Sheet of writing paper, newspaper or wrapping paper*
- ✪ *Pen or pencil*
- ✪ *Scissors*
- ✪ *Repositionable spray glue*
- ✪ *Chalk (optional)*

STENCILS

Learning to stencil was what initially gave me the confidence to do the decorative painting that I do now. Quite often it is just lack of experience and confidence in our drawing or drafting skills that hold us back from tackling ambitious projects. I have found that the way around this is to make or buy a stencil with a good basic but simple shape. A stencil made with care will provide you with the basis for many successful projects.

There are so many stencils available these days that you can buy one for practically any image. The stencils I make tend to be basic outlines of motifs, to which legs, features or other details can be added by hand.

1 Lay the acetate over the motif and carefully trace around the outer edge, using the permanent marker. (If you need to enlarge or reduce a motif, the easiest way to do this is on a photocopier that has that facility.)

TEMPLATES

For some designs, a template is easier to use than a stencil, and I have found myself becoming increasingly dependent on simple templates. They are particularly helpful when creating a motif that requires symmetry. Good examples where templates saved the day were the Ginger Jar Wall Plaques (page 98) and the Coat of Arms Mural (page 28); for the latter, I used the templates to make a symmetrical stencil. Templates work well for topiary trees, too.

1 Fold the piece of paper in half. With the pen or pencil, draw half of the desired shape, so that the fold of the paper will run down the centre of the finished template.

2 Place the acetate on the cutting mat. With the knife upright, cut out the stencil, holding the acetate with your other hand, but not in the path of the blade. To change direction, turn the acetate, rather than the knife. When removing the area you have cut around, take care not to tear the stencil shape.

3 Lightly spray the back of the stencil with repositionable spray glue. If necessary, use masking tape to mask out any parts of the stencil that will be in a different colour. (You can also use masking tape – the low-tack type – to mask out particular parts of the surface that you do not want to stencil.)

4 Place the stencil on the surface to be painted. Apply a very small amount of paint with a stencil brush. Carefully lift off the stencil. (For conventional stencilling, you could go on to stencil additional colours once the paint is dry.)

5 For my work I usually need a solid, opaque finish, instead of the soft, textured look stencilling creates. For this effect, paint over the stencilled area with a second coat of the same colour using an artist's brush.

2 Keeping the piece of paper folded, carefully cut out the half-image through both layers, then open it out to reveal the full shape. If it is either too fat or too tall, simply refold and trim with your scissors until you are happy with it.

3 Lightly spray one side with the spray glue. Lay the template on the surface to be painted and lightly draw around it with a pencil or chalk. The shape will then be ready to be filled in with paint, and the template can be used again.

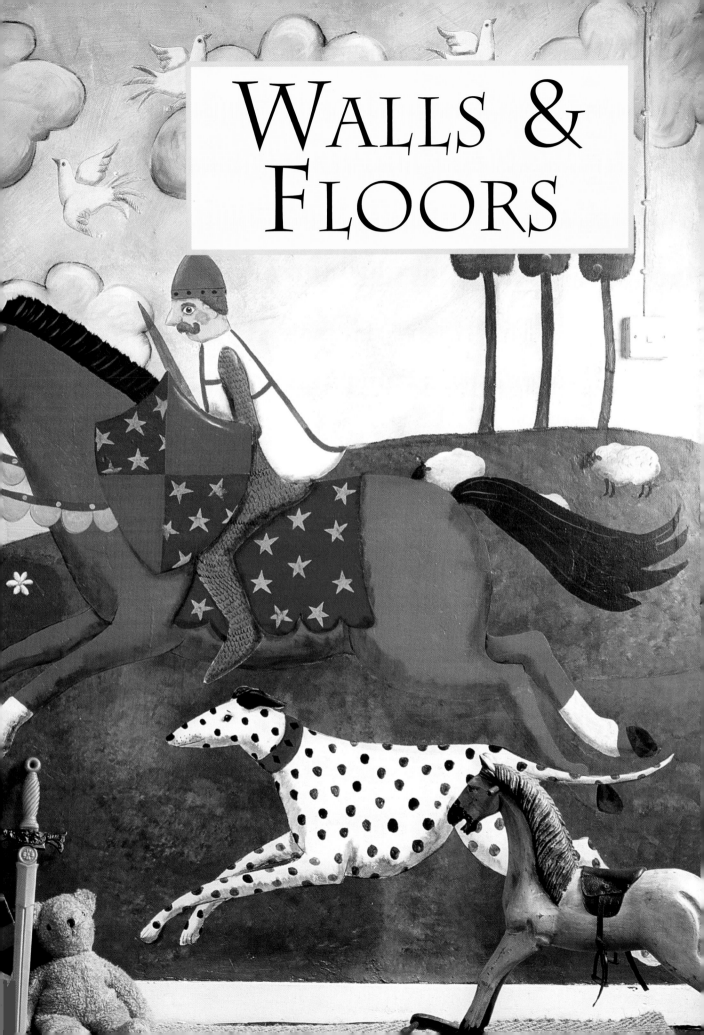

WALLS &
FLOORS

COLOURWASH

OVER THE PAST FEW YEARS colourwashes have revolutionized the task of choosing room colours. They can be particularly effective when you want a rich colour scheme but don't want the intensity of a flat colour, for example in a smaller room. The slightly rough-looking finish makes an ideal background for artwork, decorative objects and furnishings. Colourwash can also be quite forgiving on walls that are roughly plastered or that might look shabby painted in a flat colour. In my rather old house it has proved useful for camouflaging areas of wall that might otherwise have needed replastering.

As with all unfamiliar techniques it is always worthwhile practising somewhere first. You can try out different colours on a spare board, but to become confident with the technique, however simple, a complete wall is much better. Perhaps you have a garage or spare room where a wall could be used. Remember, you can always paint over it when you have finished.

There are a number of products available today to make colourwashing easier. These tend to be semi-translucent, water-based mediums to which you add your chosen colour or tint. Instructions vary from product to product. The person selling the product may be able to give you some useful tips, because they have probably had first-hand experience of it, as well as feedback from other customers. For the colourwash shown here, I mixed 2 parts water-based (ie, acrylic) scumble glaze with 1 part colour. The colour in this case was simply emulsion paint.

YOU WILL NEED

✪ *Vinyl silk emulsion in light colour, preferably white or cream (for base coat)*
✪ *Acrylic scumble glaze or colourwash mix*
✪ *Emulsion or acrylic paint in terracotta (to tint glaze or colourwash mix)*
✪ *Good-quality 8cm (3in) decorator's brush*

TERRACOTTA COLOURWASH

1 Prepare your wall by painting it with the base coat if it is not already the right colour. Leave to dry. Mix the colourwash by adding colour to the glaze or colourwash mix. Make sure you blend them together well. Dip the brush into the mixture to a depth of about 2cm (¾in) and apply to the wall. Work the colour over the wall with the brush, building up a painting rhythm that suits you. Working quite quickly will achieve the best results. Don't reload the brush until all the colour on it has gone onto the wall.

COLOUR-WASHING TIPS

1 Colourwash is applied over a base coat of vinyl silk or matt emulsion, so make sure this base coat is nice and even.

2 Always try to mix enough colourwash to do more than the whole room, because to get a match halfway through a project can be tricky. A little goes a long way but it is better to have too much than too little.

3 Practise on a large area first to get a feel for what you are doing and to familiarize yourself with the product you have chosen.

4 Use a good-quality paintbrush. This produces a much softer effect, it's easier on your arm and you won't be constantly picking bristles off the wall.

5 Either mask off your skirting boards and architraves with low-tack tape or be prepared to repaint them – colourwashing can be quite a messy business.

6 Don't judge the final effect by the results of your first small area of wall. It is the building up of colour that creates the best results.

7 If you find the colourwashed walls too dark, bright or intense, then mix another colourwash in white or cream and work this over the top of your existing walls to tone down the colour.

2 Keep going back over your brush strokes at a different angle, to create a cross-hatching effect. This prevents the brush strokes from appearing to go in the same direction. When the wall is complete, give your arm a rest and allow the colour to dry. This will take about an hour. Now go over the wall a second time, in the same colour, working as before. You will find that the effect will start to look less messy – the finish will be richer and more consistent.

23

HARLEQUIN WALL STENCIL

THIS PATTERN LENDS ITSELF to the wall of a small room or a portion of a larger room. I first used it in an inglenook fireplace and it was an effective way of introducing a little pattern into an otherwise plainly painted room. The background here consists of two coats of a fairly vivid green colourwash. When it was dry, I stencilled the harlequin pattern on top of it. The effect is straightforward but it is hard work, so do not attempt too large an area. Also, be prepared to make two or three stencils, as their edges can get clogged with dried paint, which would spoil the effect. For a pattern that is absolutely straight, you can mark out a faint pencil grid of points corresponding to the corners of the diamonds. However, I prefer the effect if it is done by eye.

YOU WILL NEED

✪ *Good-quality 8cm (3in) decorator's brush*
✪ *Vinyl silk emulsion in light colour (for base coat)*
✪ *Colourwash (see pages 22–3) in green*
✪ *Diamond stencil (see pages 122–5)*
✪ *Repositionable spray glue*
✪ *2.5cm (1in) flat brush*
✪ *Water-based paints in light green and dark green (for decoration)*
✪ *Scrap of acetate or card*

1 Using the decorator's brush, paint on the base coat and, once it is dry, the colourwash in the usual way (see page 22–3), building up the colour to the desired effect. Leave to dry.

2 Spray the back of the stencil with glue and place it in the middle of the wall. Dip the 2.5cm (1in) flat brush into both the light and dark greens then scrape off any excess. Stencil the diamond (see pages 18–19). Reposition it so the corner almost touches that of the diamond you've already done. Make sure it is straight, then proceed as before.

3 Continue in the same way, working outwards and taking particular care when repositioning the stencil. When you reach the top of the wall or a corner, bend the stencil so that it fits neatly into the right angle. Lightly spray an uncut piece of acetate or card with glue, and use it to mask out any areas you don't wish to stencil.

BIRD IN A TREE WALL PATTERN

T HIS SIMPLE BIRD in a tree looks pretty stencilled as a repeat pattern over colourwashed walls. I used two stencils to produce this image – one (consisting of two pieces of A4 acetate taped together) for the pot and tree, including the leaves and fruit, and a second for the bird. Using two stencils enables you to keep light and dark colours separate and create crisper images.

When working with two stencils that will be overlaid, as these are, it is worth tracing some of the images from the other stencil onto the one you are cutting. Do this for each stencil. These will act as register marks, helping you to position the stencils. Once you have decided on your spacing, mark a small 'X' in chalk on the wall at the point where each image will be positioned. I tend to do this by eye, but if you like your patterns absolutely even, you could measure and mark out a grid using a tape measure and a spirit level.

TIP When you are stencilling the bird, put a blob of white paint onto the acetate stencil itself, so you can pick up a small amount on your brush when needed, instead of dipping into the pot and possibly picking up too much paint.

YOU WILL NEED

❂ Chalk
❂ Repositionable spray glue
❂ Tree stencil (see pages 122–5)
❂ 3 No. 8 stencil brushes
❂ Water-based paints in terracotta, brown, black, green, yellow and white
❂ Bird stencil (see pages 122–5)
❂ No. 4 artist's brush
❂ Cutting knife (optional)

1 After marking out in chalk the positions of the motifs, spray the back of the tree stencil with glue and stick it in position on the wall. Stencil the pot and the fruits in terracotta. Using the same brush and a small amount of brown paint, stencil the tree trunk and branches. Shade around the edges of the pot and the main tree trunk with black.

2 With a new brush, stencil in the leaves, using green and yellow on the same brush. Move the stencil to the next point. When the tree is dry, spray the back of the bird stencil with glue and position it over the stencilled tree. Stencil a white bird using a clean brush. With the brush used in step 1, lightly shade the bird with black.

3 Remove the stencil carefully. When the stencilling is dry, add an eye to the bird using black paint and a No. 4 brush. Also add some fine lines to define the wings and neck. Repeat the procedure around the room. If your tree stencil starts to get clogged, use a cutting knife to open up the clogged areas, or cut a new stencil.

COAT
OF ARMS
MURAL

This sloping attic ceiling was a bit of a challenge but the results made it well worthwhile.

THIS SET OF HERALDIC shields is ideal for painting directly onto the wall of a child's room to achieve a colourful, dramatic mural. The instructions in this project are for painting the castle tower shield, but the same techniques can be used to paint the birds, fleur-de-lis, stylized lion or Maltese crosses pictured below, opposite and overleaf (for stencils, see pages 122–5). Alternatively, you could easily customize the basic design to suit the child's tastes and interests. A book on heraldry or coats of arms will offer plenty of inspiration and surprisingly simple motifs.

A set of shields grouped together looks stunning but you will need to cut all the stencils before you start to paint. To enable you to plan the design and colours, cut out a set of four mini-shields about 12cm (5in) tall, and paint them using the desired colours and motifs to see how they look together. Try varying the colour and motif combinations – for example, you could use the repeated white bird motif on a red-and-green chequerboard background.

Once you are happy with the mini-shields, make the larger templates from which to cut all the stencils. You may wish to paint more than one shield size, in which case you will need to create more than one template. If the shields are larger than A4 size, you can tape sheets of acetate together – for the ones shown, I used four pieces of A4 acetate per stencil.

This careful preparation is worth the effort, as the stencils you create can be used again for accessorizing the room with decorated furniture, lampshades and fabric. You could even use a colour photocopier to copy your mini-shields, then cut out the photocopies and glue them to accessories.

28

YOU WILL NEED

✪ *Shield stencil (see pages 122–5)*
✪ *Repositionable spray glue*
✪ *2.5cm (1in) flat brush*
✪ *Water-based paints in yellow, black, white, brown and red*
✪ *Pencil*
✪ *Ruler*
✪ *Square stencil*
✪ *Stencil brush*
✪ *Castle tower stencil (see pages 122–5)*
✪ *Nos. 1, 4 and 8 artist's brushes*
✪ *Gold paint (optional)*

1 Spray the back of the shield stencil lightly with glue and position it on the wall. Using the flat brush, apply yellow paint, working outwards from the centre of the shield. Once the paint is dry, apply a second coat for a strong opaque finish. Allow to dry. Leave the stencil in place for the next step. Rule a fine pencil line down the shield's centre.

2 Spray the back of the square stencil with glue, and place it halfway down the line, with one edge of the square against the line. Using the stencil brush, stencil in black. Move the stencil diagonally to the next position so the squares are corner to corner; repeat the process. Do the other squares in the same way. The shield stencil will keep the outline neat. Remove the stencils and leave the paint to dry.

3 Spray the back of the tower stencil with glue and position it centrally on the shield. Fill in using the stencil brush from step 2 dipped in a small amount of white paint, which will create a stone colour. Remove the stencil. When the stone colour is dry, mix a deep grey shade using black and white and apply a second coat of paint to the tower using the No. 8 brush. Leave to dry.

TIP When stencilling, make sure you don't use too much paint at the edges, or the colour could bleed underneath.

4 Draw the windows and door on the tower, then add some simple brickwork using a pencil and ruler. Paint over the lines and fill in the windows using a No. 1 brush with watered-down black paint. Fill in the door using brown paint and outline the tower with a fine black line. Outline the door with black, and add a black knocker and some black dots as studs.

5 With a pencil and ruler, draw the flagpole at the top of the tower. Paint it using a No. 1 brush and the grey paint mixture. Pencil in the flag freehand and paint it white using a No. 4 brush. When it is dry, you can add a motif to the flag – a red star or cross, or perhaps a child's initials.

6 Finally, give the tower more substance and form by shading around the edge using watered-down black paint and a No. 4 brush, then blending with your finger. Once the shield is complete, add a black or gold line around the outside as a lovely finishing touch.

ORIENTAL TROMPE L'OEIL RUG

A FAUX ORIENTAL RUG IS a fun way to brighten up wooden floorboards and can be applied to either a painted floor, as here, or bare boards. I decided to use vivid colours, which were in keeping with the room's theme, but it can be as colourful or low-key as you want. The project was quite quick to complete, although I do advise that you take care when marking out your rug initially – once it is painted, it would be quite an ordeal to move it along the floor!

This project gives you plenty of scope for different designs, which could easily be modified to suit the room it is to be painted in. Many of the designs in other projects in the book could be adapted for this rug. For example, the teddy motifs from the toy chest project would make colourful and much-loved additions to a child's bedroom or playroom. It is a good idea to start with a fairly small surface area, such as the one shown here, but when you are feeling confident, you could make a real statement and tackle a larger expanse of floor.

Finish your *trompe l'oeil* rug with a tough matt varnish to prolong its life. Although painted floors are quite hard-wearing it is a good idea to position the 'rug' in an area of relatively low traffic so that it will survive for many years.

The tassels at either end of the rug add an elegant touch, and the shading beneath gives an illusion of depth.

YOU WILL NEED

✪ *Template made from paper to the exact dimensions of your planned rug*
✪ *Chalk*
✪ *Pencil (optional)*
✪ *2.5cm (1in) flat brush*
✪ *Water-based paints in pink, terracotta, navy blue, light green, dark green and white*
✪ *Square stencil*
✪ *Repositionable spray glue*
✪ *Stencil brush*
✪ *Oriental stencil (see pages 122–5)*
✪ *Gold paint (acrylic if possible)*
✪ *Ruler*
✪ *No. 4 artist's brush*
✪ *Tassel stencil (see pages 122–5)*
✪ *Matt varnish and varnishing brush*

TIP **The gold creates quite a subtle effect. If you prefer something slightly more opaque, then use a dark colour for the diamonds but highlight them with a little gold.**

1 Make sure that your floor is clean, dry and dust free. Lay the paper template out on the floor to get the position exactly right. My template was made from two pieces of wrapping paper taped together, which I found was the exact size and shape I needed. Carefully draw around your template with chalk or a pencil.

2 Remove the template. Using the flat brush, paint in the pink base colour within the outline of your rug, taking particular care around the edges.

3 When it is dry, find the centre of the painted area. Spray glue onto the back of the square stencil and position it at an angle to make a diamond shape. Using the stencil brush, stencil it in terracotta. Stencil the remaining diamonds in the same way, positioning them corner to corner and working outwards from the centre.

4 When these are dry, spray the back of the oriental stencil with glue and position it over a point where two diamonds meet; stencil using gold paint. Repeat for the other points where diamonds meet.

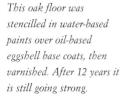

5 Rule a border all the way around the inside of the pink area, approximately 4–5cm (1½–2in) from the edge. Paint the border navy blue, using the flat brush and taking particular care at the edges. Leave to dry.

6 On the border, mark out in chalk a simple leaf pattern. Paint the leaves with the No. 4 brush using light and dark greens.

7 Spray the back of the tassel stencil with glue. Place it 2mm (¹⁄₁₆in) outside the edge of the rug at one end. Using dark green paint and a stencil brush, stencil a tassel. Move the stencil along to stencil the remaining tassels at that end, and then repeat at the other end, again placing the stencil about 2mm (¹⁄₁₆in) away from the edge of the rug.

8 Carefully fill in the tassels by hand, using the No. 4 brush and dark green paint.

9 When the tassels are dry, add a little embellishment of terracotta paint as shown, using the same brush.

10 Create a light 'shadow' under each tassel using slightly watered-down navy blue paint and the artist's brush. Still with the same brush, highlight the terracotta part of each tassel with a little white. Varnish when dry.

COUNTRY CASTLE MURAL

T HIS WAS MY FIRST attempt at a full-size mural and I discovered that there is nothing more intimidating than a blank wall expectantly awaiting a mural! It was to be in the bedroom that had the coats of arms painted on the walls (see page 28), so I knew the scene had to be something that would work with them and also appeal to a young child for at least a few years. In addition, I wanted to tackle only images I was familiar with and confident about painting. As I have a certain amount of difficulty in drawing human figures, I decided to keep these to a minimum. The resulting step-by-step photographs show how the mural progressed and evolved. I hope that they inspire you to tackle such a project yourself.

MURAL-PAINTING TIPS

1 *You will need to paint the wall a neutral colour to begin with. The background for mine was already a pale blue colourwash, which was perfect for the sky.*

2 *It is a good idea to plan out the entire mural first, even if it is just a rough sketch of the placement of various components.*

3 *Take into account any furniture that you will need to accommodate when the mural is completed.*

4 *When you start your painting, don't get discouraged. You'll see from the photographs that things don't look too promising in the beginning. Just remember that it is the build-up of detail, which happens fairly late in the process, that makes it pleasing to the eye.*

5 *Invest in a good selection of paints. Some 250ml (8fl oz) sample pots will be perfect, although you may need a little extra green and white.*

6 *Have a good number of brushes in varying sizes at your disposal. You might need to buy* some larger artist's brushes to tackle some of the bigger images.

7 *Don't let anyone discourage you. When my daughter saw the horse with its white socks, she thought that there was something wrong with it and that it was wearing bandages…so don't be put off by this sort of remark!*

8 *Make stencils for birds, fruit, flowers or other motifs when appropriate. It will save time later.*

9 *Wipe out any chalk marks with a damp cloth as you progress.*

10 *Don't overtax yourself. Rome wasn't built in a day. Try to set aside a little time – perhaps two hours – each day to work on the project, and firmly set aside your paintbrush (washed, of course!) at the end of the allotted time. You don't want to get mural burn-out.*

11 *When finished, apply a coat of acrylic eggshell varnish. It gives a nice soft sheen to the wall but you can still paint over it if you wish to add some more details at a later stage.*

1 Paint the wall with the vinyl silk emulsion if it is not already the right colour. When it is dry, use chalk to mark out roughly the landscape of your mural, deciding how much sky and how much ground you need. Draw in clouds, trees and architectural features. Once you are happy with the landscape, go over the outlines with black pastel crayon. The black pastel outline is not strictly necessary – I did it so the outlines would show up in the photo and then found that it enhanced the overall effect.

2 Paint any ground area in green using a 4cm (1¹⁄₂in) flat brush. This can be quite rough, as it is just a background for grass. When dry, use the same brush to stipple (dab) both green and yellow paint roughly onto the green background.

39

3 Fill in the tree trunks, using brown and black together on a 2cm (³/₄in) flat brush to create natural-looking 'bark'.

4 With the 2cm (³/₄in) flat brush, fill in the clouds with white paint. Shade the undersides of the clouds slightly, using the same brush and slightly watered-down black paint, then blend it roughly into the white for a neutral look.

5 Add terracotta-coloured fruits to the trees, either stencilling or hand-painting them with a No. 6 brush. With the same size brush, shade the undersides, highlight each fruit with white, then add leaves using yellow and green together. For the trees in the background, simply stipple greenery on top of the trunks in the same way as you painted the grass in step 2. When dry, paint some small terracotta-coloured fruits on them using a No. 4 brush.

6 With a 2cm (³/₄in) flat brush and a No. 6 brush for the edges, fill in the grey tower. When dry, paint the door brown using the No. 6 brush. When that is dry, add black studs and a door-handle using a No. 4 brush. Fill in the windows with a black wash, using the No. 6 brush. Add brickwork using a No. 4 brush and slightly watered-down black paint.

7 Either stencil or use the No. 4 brush to paint some white daisies. When dry, add the yellow centres. There don't need to be too many of these daisies but a scattering around the base of the tower is pretty.

8 Either stencil or use the No. 6 brush to paint white sheep shapes; as they dry, shade them with slightly watered-down black, blending it in with your finger. When dry, use the No. 4 brush to add black faces and legs to complete the detailing.

9 Chalk in a pig family. Remember that you can keep drawing and wiping out chalk lines until you are happy with your pigs. Using a No. 6 brush, fill in the shapes with beige paint.

10 Stencil or use a No. 6 brush to paint white doves. When dry, apply a second coat. When those are dry, add yellow beaks and eyes and black detailing using a No. 4 brush. With the same brush, shade the doves.

11 Using the No. 4 brush, add black spots, eyes and eyebrows, snouts, knees and trotters to your pig family.

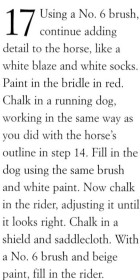

15 When dry, chalk in the forelock, mane and tail – a tail streaming out behind the horse adds real movement and life to the scene. Use a 2cm (³/₄in) flat brush to fill these in with black, and leave to dry.

16 With the No. 6 brush, fill in some of the black details, such as the eye, mouth, nostril, hooves and ears. Highlight the eye, forelock, mane and tail with white.

17 Using a No. 6 brush, continue adding detail to the horse, like a white blaze and white socks. Paint in the bridle in red. Chalk in a running dog, working in the same way as you did with the horse's outline in step 14. Fill in the dog using the same brush and white paint. Now chalk in the rider, adjusting it until it looks right. Chalk in a shield and saddlecloth. With a No. 6 brush and beige paint, fill in the rider.

12 Shade your pigs with slightly watered-down black paint, using the No. 6 brush and blending it in with your finger. Outline them in black using the No. 4 brush.

13 Shade the edges of the daisies in the same way, so that they blend into the background slightly.

14 Chalk a horse onto the wall in an appropriate place. Be bold! If you didn't plan your mural carefully at the beginning, you might need to cover up something that you have already painted. As you can see, my horse wiped out almost an entire flock of sheep! Using a 2cm (³/₄in) flat brush, fill in the horse with brown paint, shading the underside with slightly watered-down black and blending it in with your finger.

18 When dry, use a No. 6 brush to fill in grey chain-mail, a grey cap, a white tabard and a red shield, plus a red collar on the dog.

19 When it is dry, divide the shield into quadrants using chalk lines. Continue working on the horse's and knight's livery, painting the saddlecloth in dark blue using a No. 6 brush. There is a lot of scope for design and colour here. On the dog, add bold black spots and details such as eye, nose, mouth, ear, feet and collar studs, using a No. 6 brush.

20 Using Nos. 4 and 6 brushes, add details to the knight's face in terracotta, dark blue, black and white. Use the No. 4 brush to outline his tabard in red, and to paint rows of 'squiggles' on the chain-mail using watered-down black paint. Fill in two diagonally opposite quadrants on the shield with dark blue, using a No. 6 brush. Add yellow dots to the horse's bridle and yellow scallops to the reins with a No. 4 brush. With the No. 6 brush, paint in a grey sword. Stencil yellow stars on the shield and saddlecloth. Highlight the bridle, shield and knight's cap with white, using a No. 4 brush. Shade the lower edges of the knight and the dog using slightly watered-down black paint and a No. 6 brush. To fill a gap, I added a cow. I also gave the knight a 'love interest' in the tower.

FURNITURE

GOOSE & EGG COFFEE TABLE

THERE IS SOMETHING ABOUT GEESE that makes them irresistible. It may be their graceful elongated shape, or perhaps their slightly bemused expression. At any rate, they make ideal motifs for country painting and look lovely decorating a variety of objects. For this project I found an oblong coffee table in untreated white wood which was perfect for painting in water-based paints. To give an existing table a facelift, simply paint on a base coat of mid-sheen oil-based paint, allow it to dry and then proceed from step 2.

My intention was to keep the colours cool, pale and light, to go with the white geese and the creamy-coloured eggs. The design is quite simple and requires only two stencils, one for the goose and one for the eggs. The goose stencil needs to be fairly large – for mine, I taped two sheets of acetate together. Painting the geese's legs, feet and beaks shouldn't present a problem if you draw them first in chalk, adjusting the outlines until you feel that the proportions are right.

As an alternative design, you could stencil the oriental motif in gold on a blue base coat, then paint a trellis of fruit and leaves plus a leafy border, and finally stencil or paint doves or flowers on it.

If you want a slightly darker, antique finish, you can apply antiquing liquid (either water-based or oil-based) prior to varnishing it. I wanted to keep the colours light and fresh, so I used just a clear acrylic varnish with an eggshell finish. Varnish is essential on an item like this – a table will often have glasses, hot drinks and food placed on it, not to mention small sticky fingers, unable to resist the images.

YOU WILL NEED

✪ *Coffee table preferably in untreated, white wood*

✪ *2.5cm (1in) flat brush*

✪ *Water-based paints in pale blue (for base coat) and pale green (for border)*

✪ *Fine-grade sandpaper*

✪ *Clean cloth*

✪ *Ruler*

✪ *Pencil*

✪ *Repositionable spray glue*

✪ *Goose stencil (see pages 48–9)*

✪ *Stencil brush*

✪ *Water-based paints in white, yellow, beige, black and terracotta (for decoration)*

✪ *Nos. 1, 4 and 6 artist's brushes*

✪ *Chalk*

✪ *Egg stencil (see pages 48–9)*

✪ *Antiquing liquid, 2.5cm (1in) varnishing brush and soft cloth (optional)*

✪ *Clear eggshell acrylic varnish*

1 Using the flat brush, paint your table in the pale blue base coat. It is a good idea to start by turning the table over onto its back so that you have easier access to the legs. When completely dry, sand lightly with fine-grade sandpaper, then dust it down with a damp cloth.

2 Using a ruler and a pencil, mark out a border approximately 4cm (1½in) from the edge all the way around the table. With the flat brush and pale green paint, fill in the border you have marked out. You'll need to take particular care when painting along the inner line, but you can always touch up with pale blue when the green is dry.

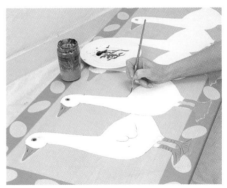

5 Spray the back of the egg stencil with glue, and position the stencil within the border of the table. Stencil beige eggs all around the border, changing the angle of the egg slightly each time. For the eggs around the geese's feet, overlap egg over foot sometimes and foot over egg at other times.

6 Use a No. 6 brush to paint over the stencilled eggs with another coat of beige paint. When dry, use the No. 4 brush and black paint to add details such as the nostril, mouth, eye, wing, legs and lines on the feet to each goose. Add a fine line of watered-down black paint all around the edge of each goose to make it stand out.

TIP **To stencil an egg so that an already painted foot overlaps it, first stencil the egg over the painted foot and then paint the foot again over the egg.**

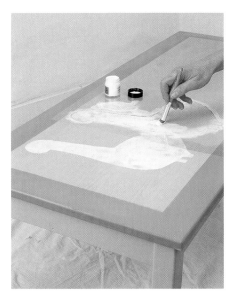

3 Lightly spray the back of the goose stencil with glue and carefully place it in its first position on the left side of the tabletop. Stencil the goose with white paint, taking particular care around the edges. When dry, lift the stencil off and move it a short distance so that the chest of the second goose overlaps the front goose's tail. Continue in this way until you reach the end of the table.

4 Use a No. 6 brush to paint over the stencilled areas with another coat of white paint. When dry, chalk in beaks, legs and feet and adjust the outline until you are happy with the proportions. (For more detail, study the illustration on pages 48–9.) With the No. 6 brush and yellow paint, fill in the chalk outlines. Add a yellow eye to each goose with the No. 4 brush.

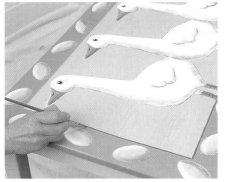

7 Carefully shade the eggs and the geese, using watered-down black paint and the No. 4 brush and then blend it in with your fingertip. Don't forget to shade the geese's legs and feet. Try to keep this soft and subtle.

8 Still using the No.4 brush, add bold white highlights to the eggs and a white dot on each goose's eye. Now paint a 2mm-(¹⁄₁₆in-) wide line between the green border and the blue base colour, using the same brush and slightly watered-down terracotta paint. When it is all dry, sand lightly and dust it down with a damp cloth. Paint on antiquing liquid if desired, wiping off excess. When dry, apply a coat of varnish.

TIP Try to shade the eggs and geese as lightly as possible to begin with, as it is important not to make the black too heavy on light colours like these.

PAINTED ARTS & CRAFTS SCREEN

WILLIAM MORRIS AND THE other designers of the Arts & Crafts Movement were famous for their free-flowing designs incorporating repeat patterns of animal motifs against backgrounds of twining branches. For this Arts & Crafts-inspired screen, I used stencilled motifs of a rabbit, a dog and a bird, all linked by leafy branches of fruit. The black background sets off the colours and allows the screen to fit into a period setting.

Although I had never painted a full-size screen before, I was immediately inspired by this screen's elegant panels, with their lovely scalloped tops. One of the great recent excitements for all decorative artists has been the superb choice of imaginative and inexpensive 'blanks' to paint. These are usually made from MDF (medium-density fibreboard), which lacks the knots, grain and general character of wood but is an excellent medium for decorative painting and découpage. It requires little or no preparation and is quickly transformed from dull beige to something as colourful and exciting as you are prepared to tackle.

With a large project such as this, remember to allow yourself plenty of time. Although the steps are simple and straightforward, there is a good deal of repetitive work. Once you have cut the stencils, practise stencilling each of the main motifs on paper or wood first. This will make it less daunting when you come to apply them. And when you have finished the screen, if you are feeling ambitious, you could tackle the other side!

The important finishing touches to the screen are visible here. The gold edging with a painted red line is a handsome border for the main design.

YOU WILL NEED

- ✪ *Three-panel MDF screen*
- ✪ *Clean cloth*
- ✪ *Water-based paint in black (for base coat)*
- ✪ *4cm (¹/₂in) flat brush*
- ✪ *Dog stencil (see pages 54–5)*
- ✪ *Dove stencil (see pages 54–5)*
- ✪ *Rabbit stencil (see pages 54–5)*
- ✪ *Fruit stencil (see pages 54–5)*
- ✪ *Repositionable spray glue*
- ✪ *Stencil brush*
- ✪ *Water-based paints in white, brown, red, black, terracotta, green and yellow (for decoration)*
- ✪ *Nos. 1, 4, and 8 artist's brushes*
- ✪ *Chalk (optional)*
- ✪ *Gold paint*
- ✪ *Fine-grade sandpaper*
- ✪ *Antiquing liquid, 2.5cm (1in) varnishing brush and soft cloth*
- ✪ *Satin varnish*

TIP **I prefer to position stencils by eye rather than by measuring. If you fix the stencil to the screen with spray glue then stand back and check that it is not crooked, you should be able to judge whether the placement is right. When you are happy with it, you can stencil the animals.**

1 Wipe the screen down with a slightly damp, clean cloth to remove any MDF dust, then start applying the black base colour using the flat brush. Two coats will be necessary. By the time you have finished painting the last panel, the first panel should be ready to receive its second coat. Leave this to dry, too.

2 Use a different stencil for each panel, spraying the backs with glue and then stencilling the dogs and doves in white and the rabbit in brown. Use the paint sparingly to prevent it from seeping under the stencil. At the edges of each panel, you can stencil just a portion of the animal.

3 When dry, paint over each of the stencilled areas with another coat of the same colour, using the No. 8 brush for the main body and the No. 4 brush for the more fiddly areas such as the legs and tails. Leave to dry.

6 Shade all the stencilled motifs using slightly watered-down black paint and the No. 4 brush, blending it in lightly with your fingertips.

7 Highlight each image – animals and fruit – with a dab of white paint, again using the No. 4 brush and blending with your finger. Don't forget to dot the animals' eyes, using the No. 1 brush (but do not blend in this highlight).

8 Join the fruits together with loose, curving strokes, chalking in the lines first if you wish and then painting them brown using the No. 8 brush. Keep the lines quite evenly spread out, as the leaves will cover most of them.

4 With the No. 4 brush, add detail to the motifs. On the dogs I used red for the collars and black for the eyes, ears, mouths and noses, for the lines defining parts of the body and, of course, for the spots. Refer to the illustration on pages 54–5 for more detail.

5 Stencil in terracotta fruits in the same manner as the main motifs. When dry, paint over the stencilled areas with another coat of terracotta paint, using the No. 8 brush.

TIP I often add an inner coloured line to a gold border, as here. It not only looks good but also covers up any rough edges.

9 Add the foliage using the No. 8 brush dipped into both green and yellow to add lustre to the leaves. If you feel that the foliage is too sparse in places, simply add another branch or tip of a branch and paint more leaves onto that. Don't worry if the leaves cover parts of the motifs.

10 Add a gold border to each of your panels. I painted mine free-hand using the No. 8 brush, and it came out fairly uniform all the way around. However, the next step makes the gold look charmingly wobbly, setting off the pretty, curved shape of the screen.

11 Using a No. 4 brush, paint a narrow red border along the inside edge of the gold border. When dry, apply a second coat. Lightly sand the panels, especially around the edges. Wipe down with a damp cloth. When dry, apply an antiquing liquid. When this is dry, apply a coat of varnish.

PINEAPPLE BEDSIDE CABINET

APOPULAR FOLK-ART MOTIF, the pineapple is an age-old symbol of hospitality. I wanted to decorate a bedside cabinet for a guest bedroom, so this theme was ideal. Painting a pineapple was a new venture for me, but once I had got the shape right, I was satisfied with the way the colours and textures built up. To fill the space around the pineapple, I stencilled a simple oriental repeat pattern which adds to the whole effect of the piece.

Precut pineapple stencils are quite widely available, but because I was unable to find one the right size for the cabinet, I cut one myself. Cutting your own stencils is no problem, especially if you make templates first, following the instructions on pages 18–19. They are quick and easy to make and a good way of getting the size exactly right for your particular piece of furniture.

The bedside cabinet started life as a simple white-wood cabinet and so was a perfect candidate for painting with water-based paints. If you are painting an old piece of furniture, however, you could use a mid-sheen, satin or eggshell oil-based background colour. I replaced the knobs that came on the cabinet with some slightly more interesting ceramic ones. The use of gold paint also makes it much more exotic, but the pineapple motifs are what really have the impact. If you follow the steps carefully, you should be able to produce pineapples that look good enough to eat.

The oriental motif stencilled in gold provides a rich background pattern for the exotic pineapple painted on the door of the bedside cabinet.

YOU WILL NEED

- Bedside cabinet
- Medium-grade sandpaper (optional)
- Clean cloth
- Water-based or oil-based paint in mint green (for base coat)
- 2.5cm (1in) flat brush
- Oriental stencil (see pages 122–5)
- Repositionable spray glue
- Gold acrylic paint (for oriental motifs and trim)
- Stencil brush
- Pineapple stencil (see pages 60–1)
- Water-based paints in green, amber (see Tip), yellow, brown, black and white (for pineapples)
- Nos. 1, 4 and 6 artist's brushes
- Chalk or pencil (optional)
- Fine-grade sandpaper
- Antiquing liquid, 2.5 (1in) varnishing brush and soft cloth

1 Remove the knobs on the cabinet, and prepare the surface according to the finish it already has. If you feel that it would benefit from a light sanding before you paint it, go ahead and do so with a medium-grade sandpaper. Wipe down the surface with a damp cloth, then apply the mint green base coat with the flat brush. Remove the drawer and paint only its fascia, not the sides. Allow the paint to dry, then apply a second coat.

2 When the base coat is completely dry, spray the back of the oriental stencil with glue. Position it centrally on one side, and stencil with the gold acrylic paint. Stencil the remaining motifs on that side so that they radiate out from the central one, forming a repeat pattern. There's no need to measure – just judge with your eye. Repeat for the other side of the cabinet, as well as the front and the top.

6 Using brown paint and a No. 4 brush, paint some brown lines across the fruit diagonally in both directions, for a cross-hatching effect. (You can chalk or pencil them in first if you prefer.)

7 When the lines are dry, fill in the segments between them with yellow paint using the same brush. Occasionally dip it into the amber with which you stencilled the fruit, as this will add depth and texture.

8 When dry, add a little brown 'star' in the centre of each segment, still using the No. 4 brush. Your pineapple should now be starting to look quite realistic.

3 When the gold stencil pattern has dried, spray the pineapple stencil with glue and position it centrally on one side. It doesn't matter if it overlaps the oriental motifs. Stencil using green for the leaves and amber for the fruit. Repeat for the other side, front and top.

4 Fill in the fruit with a No. 6 brush and the same amber paint to give it a denser, more opaque finish than the stencilling produces.

5 Fill in the leaves using the No. 6 brush and the same green paint as you stencilled with, plus a little yellow. Using the green and yellow together on the brush creates an attractive, varied texture. Don't forget the leaves at the bottom.

TIP **In the water-based paints used for the pineapple, 'amber' means a colour midway between brown and yellow, so a mixture of the two would suffice.**

9 Shade the fruit and leaves with watered-down black paint and a No. 4 brush, especially on the underside of the fruit. You can also use the black paint on a No. 1 brush to define the leaves. Highlight the fruit and leaves with white paint and a No. 4 brush.

10 Add gold acrylic to any appropriate areas. On this bedside cabinet, the feet lent themselves to being embellished, and around the drawer and door there were natural borders which were ideal for being painted gold.

11 Lightly rub down your piece of furniture using fine-grade sandpaper, distressing the edges. Dust it down with the damp cloth. Finally, paint on antiquing liquid, work it into all the corners and then wipe it off with a soft cloth.

YOU WILL NEED

✪ *Suitable bed for painting*
✪ *Water- or oil-based paint in light blue (for base colour)*
✪ *2.5cm (1in) flat brush*
✪ *Paper for template*
✪ *Repositionable spray glue*
✪ *Elephant stencil (see pages 66–7; also step 2, right, before cutting)*
✪ *Stencil brush*
✪ *Water-based paints in grey, white, yellow, black, pink, light green and dark green (for decoration)*
✪ *Daisy stencil (see pages 122–5)*
✪ *Nos. 1, 4 and 6 artist's brushes*
✪ *Chalk*
✪ *Gold paint*
✪ *Satin varnish and varnishing brush*

1 Carefully paint your bed with the base coat, using the flat brush. Remember that, in order to be long-lasting, it should be well prepared and the paint applied with care. Try not to miss any hidden crevices. A second coat after the first has dried is recommended. Leave to dry.

2 Before cutting the elephant stencil, make a simple paper template of it so that you can check the elephant's proportions in relation to the bed. Spray it with glue, position it on the bedhead then check that the motifs will neither over-power nor be swamped by the bed. Check how it looks on the tailboard, too. You can then cut the stencil.

3 Spray the back of the elephant stencil with glue, and position it on the headboard. Carefully stencil the elephant using a stencil brush and grey paint. Repeat the design where appro-priate – I have applied the design to both sides of the tailboard as well as to the headboard.

7 Paint the blanket and face decoration in pink, using the No. 6 brush. When dry, chalk a trellis pattern over both, using diagonal lines running from corner to corner. Carefully paint over the chalk lines in light green, with the No. 4 brush. Use the same brush to add light green tassels to the corners of the blanket.

8 Using your daisy stencil again, stencil a white daisy in the centre of the blanket, over the green. With the No. 4 brush, hand-paint small white daisies in the diamonds formed by the green trellis pattern on the blanket. Add even smaller white daisies to the face decoration. Use chalk to give the elephant a pair of tusks, then fill in the tusks in white, still using the No. 4 brush.

9 With the No. 1 brush, fill in the centres of all the daisies on the blanket and face decoration with yellow. Using slightly watered-down black paint and a No. 4 brush, shade the elephant. Pay particular attention around the ear and under the tail, and don't forget to shade his tusks. Add some shading to the tassels, and pick out all the large daisy motifs with a little shading around the petals and the yellow centres, using the No. 4 brush.

4 Using white paint, stencil daisies at equidistant points across the bed. Stencil the central daisy only as far as the elephant's back, so that it will look like it is actually behind the elephant.

5 When all your stencilled images have been completed, fill in each of them with the same colour as it was stencilled in. You will probably need to use a No. 4 brush for the daisies and a No. 6 brush for the elephant motif.

6 Using the No. 4 brush, paint a yellow centre on each daisy. Chalk in the detail that you will be adding to the elephant shape, such as the blanket, face decoration, toes, ear and eye. When you are happy with these, lightly paint over the lines in a slightly watered-down black paint, using the No. 4 brush.

TIP **When positioning the elephant on the bedhead, take into account the pillow and bedding; you won't want your artwork obscured by them.**

10 Using the No. 1 artist's brush and white paint, highlight each daisy centre, the elephant's ears and back, and the tassels. Dot the elephant's eye with white, too. Using the chalk, join the daisies in the border with a line following the curve of the headboard or tailboard (assuming it is curved). With a No. 4 artist's brush, paint a dark green line over the chalk line and then add dark green leaves at regular intervals.

11 Gold adds a nice finishing touch to this project. I have used it along the top of the headboard and tailboard and also on the top of the bedposts, applying it with a No. 6 brush. When all the paint is dry, protect your work with a coat of satin varnish.

ACCESSORIES & FABRICS

MINIATURE
ORIENTAL
CHEST

THIS PROJECT IS A deceptively easy one, requiring time more than artistic skill, as the patterns are all abstract and are just repeated in blocks over the miniature chest of drawers.

These widely available chests have finger holes for opening the drawers, but if you turn the drawers around, it allows you to add the knobs of your choice. Doing this immediately gives the piece more of a presence. Some time ago I had purchased these pretty ceramic oriental knobs in a gift shop and I'm delighted finally to have found the right piece on which to show them off. If you can't find ceramic knobs, then buy some small wooden ones from a DIY shop and paint them, too.

There is infinite scope for variations on this project. You can keep it very simple or let your imagination and your paintbrush run wild.

For this chest, I made six different patterns – one for each drawer. I then divided the top and sides of the chest into quarters and copied the drawer patterns onto them, using each one twice. Gather together as many colours of paint as possible for this. Decorate one drawer at a time, building up the patterns until you are happy with them. It is the final juxtaposition of colour and pattern that makes this miniature chest so original and individual.

The following steps are just a guideline for how to start the piece. You will then need to refer to the painted artwork on page 74 – or if you are feeling inspired, create your own patterns. You may find that you are surrounded by inspiring patterns for a piece like this. Take a close look at patterned tiles, especially old ones, as well as ceramics and fabrics. All may hold simple motifs that could be reinterpreted on your chest of drawers.

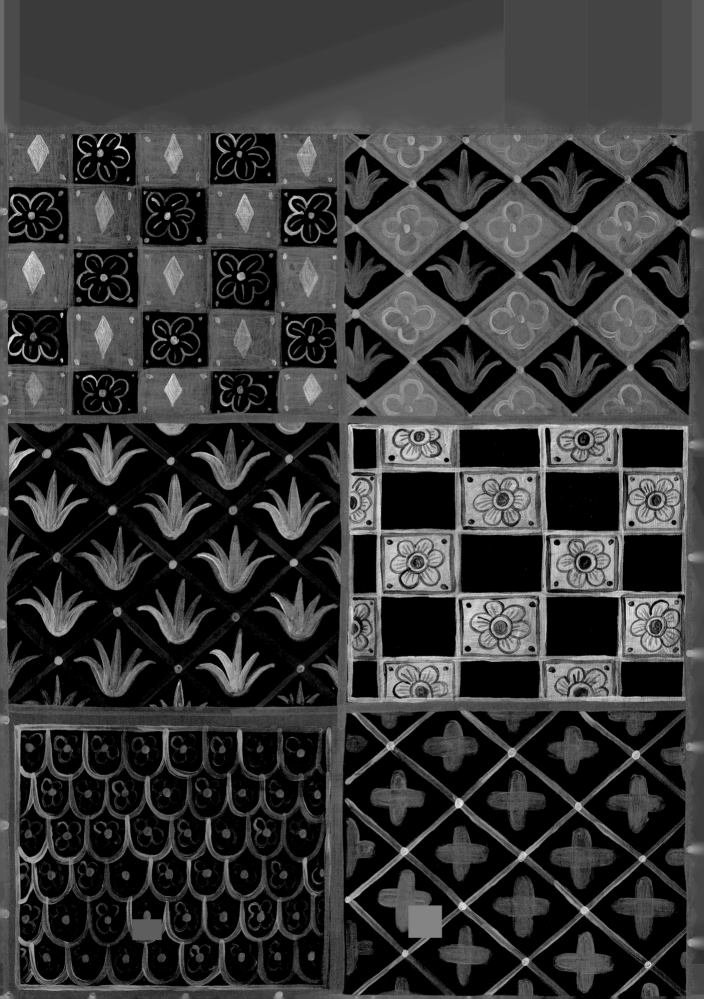

YOU WILL NEED

- ✪ *Mini-chest, with 4 or 6 drawers*
- ✪ *Fine-grade sandpaper*
- ✪ *Clean cloth*
- ✪ *2.5cm (1in) flat brush*
- ✪ *Emulsion paint in black or other dark colour (for base coat)*
- ✪ *Water-based paints in assorted colours including red, white, blue and yellow (for decoration)*
- ✪ *Nos. 1 and 4 artist's brushes*
- ✪ *Pencil*
- ✪ *Ruler*
- ✪ *4 or 6 ceramic or wooden knobs*
- ✪ *Bradawl (for making holes for knobs)*
- ✪ *Eraser*
- ✪ *Antiquing liquid, 2cm (¾in) varnishing brush and soft cloth*
- ✪ *Satin-finish polyurethane varnish*

> TIP **When painting your white grid of lines, don't be too concerned if the grid looks irregular.**

1 Sand down the mini-chest to remove any rough areas, and dust it down with a damp cloth. With the flat brush, apply the dark base coat. Leave to dry. Turn the drawers around and paint what used to be the backs and will now be the fronts. Allow to dry and then rub lightly with fine-grade sandpaper again, once more dusting it down afterwards. The smoother the surface onto which you are painting, the easier it will be.

2 Begin your first drawer. Using a No. 4 brush, paint a 6mm (¼in) red border following the edge of the drawer. When the paint is dry, go over it with a second coat, and leave that to dry.

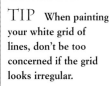

3 Using a No. 1 brush and white paint, paint a finer line along the inner edge of the red border. Now paint horizontal and vertical white lines across the drawer. Fill in alternate squares with white paint and your No. 4 brush. Allow to dry.

4 Using a sharp pencil, draw a very simple flower shape within each white square. You can see this motif most clearly in the illustration opposite. When you have drawn all the flowers, paint over them using the No. 1 brush dipped into a little watered-down blue paint (this makes the brush flow better). Try to use a light hand and pretend that you are 'writing' with your paintbrush. Continue until you have built up the blue flowers in the white squares and embellished them to your satisfaction.

This is a slightly simpler version of the project illustrated on page 73. A simple repetitive pattern is carried across all the drawers and, in different colours, over the sides and top of the chest. The knobs are simple wooden ones painted gold. The white 'banner' above each drawer provides an area for labelling the drawer contents (for example, different spices).

5 On top of the red border, add a thin yellow line with simple yellow leaves appearing to grow out of it, using the No. 1 brush dipped into slightly watered-down yellow paint.

6 When the first drawer is finished, find where the knob will eventually go by very lightly ruling two pencil lines between diagonally opposite corners; the hole for the knob should go where the two lines cross.

7 Divide each side and the top of the mini-chest into quarters. You can use a ruler and pencil but there is no need to bother measuring.

8 You can now decorate one of the quarters in the same way as the drawer. Begin by using the No. 4 brush to create the red border along the pencil lines and edges of the chest. Leave to dry.

TIP Painting the sides of the drawers means that when the drawers are pulled out they still look attractive.

9 Create the white chequerboard effect as before (step 3) and, when dry, add the blue flowers and remaining decoration (as in steps 4 and 5). Paint the insides of the drawers – a contrasting colour is a nice touch. If the knobs are wooden, paint them too. When dry, lightly sand the drawers and box, especially the corners and edges. Using the bradawl, make holes for the knobs, then rub out any pencil marks. Dust the chest down with a damp cloth. Lightly brush on antiquing liquid, removing excess with a soft cloth. When dry, add a coat of varnish and, when this has dried, add the knobs.

LEAFY
LAMP BASE
& SHADE

This lamp base was one I painted during my 'Auricula Period'. The oil-based background colour is a rich blue. Because stencilling a curved surface is tricky, I painted the design by hand, using water-based paints. I then embellished it with oil-based gold paint and varnished it with polyurethane gloss.

ERAMIC LAMP BASES IN all shapes and sizes are now widely available and are a perfect item to paint and decorate. Alternatively, if you don't want to buy a new lamp, this project is ideal for breathing new life into an old lamp base and shade that have seen better days. You will be amazed at how you can transform a plain, shabby bedside lamp, for example.

You will need to use an oil-based paint for the base coat, but once this has dried you can decorate the lamp base in any way you wish using water-based paints. I have done this a number of times and find that the hand-painted lamps make a lovely addition to any room in the house, and it would be quite easy to adapt the pattern and colour of your design to suit the room it is destined for.

I've chosen a simple leaf design for this project because it can be adapted to virtually any room setting. If the lamp's shade is quite plain and is made from either card or a fabric which has a fairly close weave, you could add some matching decoration to the shade too, as shown.

When painting the decoration onto the prepared lamp base, remember to put the central motif, if there is one, on the front; in other words, the electrical flex should be at the back. It is best to plan the design for your lampshade very carefully, because once the paint is on, you cannot remove it or paint over it.

1 Prepare the lamp base by applying mid-sheen oil-based paint, painting it on evenly using the flat brush and watching out for drips and runs. Leave to dry. If the lamp base was a similar colour to the base coat, you may not need to apply a second coat. If the base colour looks streaky, then add a second coat and allow to dry.

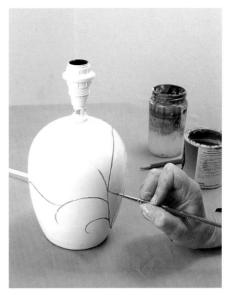

2 When the lamp base is completely dry, pencil in your design. Use quite a loose, free hand to create branches for the leaves, covering as much of the lamp base as possible. Go over your pencil lines with brown paint using a No. 4 brush.

TIP **This will work best if the lamp base is in a similar shade to your base coat.**

3 Dip the same brush into both light and dark green paint, and make leaves along your branches. They should be quite long and pointy. When you have covered the whole of the lamp base, check to see that there aren't any bare patches that need filling. If you find some, add extra leaves as necessary. If you feel that the lamp base needs more colour, you could tuck some fruit in among the foliage.

4 To paint the lampshade, draw a light pencil line all the way around the base of the shade about 2.5cm (1in) from the edge, and then again around the top of the shade the same distance from that edge. Using the No. 4 brush, carefully paint a brown line along each pencil line, taking care not to smudge the paint. Add leaves at regular points along the top and bottom of both lines, working all the way around the shade.

TREE &
BIRDHOUSE
FIRESCREEN

A FIRESCREEN IS ANOTHER USEFUL item that comes as an MDF (medium-density fibreboard) 'blank'. Not only is a firescreen a good way of covering up an open fireplace when not in use, but the hinged type also provides no less than three different opportunities for decorative painting! The challenge is to come up with motifs that look good individually on the three panels but at the same time work together as an overall design. I spent quite a while planning the decoration for this firescreen and found that the birdhouse motif lent itself perfectly to the side panels while the topiary tree made a nice bold image in the middle.

As usual there is a lot of scope for customizing your project by modifying the motifs. You could, for example, use lemons as your fruit, or you could change the blue-and-white patterned pot to a plain terracotta one. I couldn't resist adding the doves as they stop the design from being too symmetrical and are a pretty touch. It is worthwhile making two or three different dove stencils for this project so that

As in other projects, the gold edging sets off the elegant shape of the firescreen.

they can be either sitting, flying to the right or flying to the left.

Preparation in advance does help. Using a photocopier to enlarge or reduce the templates for the 'castle' and 'château' birdhouses and the topiary tree (see pages 84–5 and 126) allows you to adjust the size to fit your firescreen; once these paper templates are right, the birdhouses can be made into stencils. For the topiary tree you can just draw around the template onto the firescreen.

YOU WILL NEED

✪ *Three-panel MDF firescreen*
✪ *Water-based paint in parchment or off-white (for base coat)*
✪ *2cm (¾in) or 2.5cm (1in) flat brush*
✪ *2 birdhouse stencils (see page 126)*
✪ *Topiary tree template (see pages 84–5)*
✪ *Repositionable spray glue*
✪ *Pencil*
✪ *Water-based paints in black, white, brown, terracotta, yellow, dark blue, green and red (for decoration)*
✪ *Stencil brush*
✪ *Nos. 1, 4 and 6 artist's brushes*
✪ *Ruler*
✪ *Dove stencils (see pages 84–5)*
✪ *Gold paint*
✪ *Antiquing liquid, 2.5cm (1in) varnishing brush and soft cloth*
✪ *Satin varnish*

1 Paint the entire fire-screen in the parchment or off-white base colour, using the flat brush. When dry, apply a second coat, so that you have an opaque, even background on which to paint your design.

2 When the background colour is dry, spray the backs of both the birdhouse stencils and the tree template with glue and position them on the panels. Draw around the tree template with a pencil. Mix black with white to make grey, and use this to stencil the castle birdhouse. Stencil the château birdhouse in white. Carefully remove the stencils and template. Allow to dry.

3 Dilute some brown paint with a little water and use this wash and a No. 6 brush to roughly fill in the topiary balls and the tree trunk. Using the same brush, paint the pot white and give the château shape another coat of white. When dry, paint the two turrets grey and add grey lines along the pointed roof, then give the stencilled castle another coat of grey.

7 Spray the dove stencils with glue, and position them on all three panels. For each dove, stencil in white, remove the stencil and, when dry, apply another coat using a No. 4 brush. Also use white to fill in the flag on the château. When each dove is dry, use a No. 1 brush to add a yellow eye and beak and then, when these are dry, black detailing on them. With the same brush, paint in a fine outline and some wing and tail feathers using slightly watered-down black.

8 With a pencil, sketch in the pattern on the pot, and then fill in with slightly watered-down dark blue paint using the No. 4 brush. The main design here is based on diagonal squares in a chequerboard pattern, with simple fleur-de-lis motifs in the white squares.

9 Using watered-down black paint and a No. 4 brush, shade the pot and also the birdhouses, doves and fruits, blending the shading with your finger. With white paint and a No. 1 brush, highlight the château turrets, birdhouse stands, and tree fruits, again blending with your finger. Highlight the birds' eyes without blending.

TIP **To stencil doves facing both ways, either cut another stencil or clean the paint off the first stencil and then turn it over.**

4 Use a ruler and pencil to create the birdhouse stand on each side panel. Rule as straight a line as possible running from the centre of the château/castle base to about 2cm (¾in) from the base of the fire-screen panel. Pencil in the curved supports and, when you are happy with them, paint them using slightly watered-down black paint and a No. 4 brush.

5 The No. 4 brush is used to add detail to both birdhouses. Pencil in the doors and windows, then fill in with a black wash. Pencil in the outline of the front step on both, the outlines of the towers on the castle, plus a flagpole with flag and some tiles on the château roof. Paint the flagpole with black, and the other lines with the black wash, using the No. 1 brush.

6 Paint in the oranges on the topiary tree using a No. 4 brush and terracotta paint (or yellow paint if you are having lemons rather than oranges on your tree).

TIP The finish on the firescreen is antiquing liquid, but for an even more antiqued look you could use crackle varnish, following the manufacturer's instructions.

10 Using a No. 4 brush, fill in the tree trunk with a slightly less diluted brown than you used in step 3. You need only do this between the topiary balls and at the base. The leaves are added using the No. 4 brush dipped into green and yellow paints. Starting at the top edge of the top ball, add foliage around the outside and then work it in around the fruit until you have a fairly dense coverage. There will be areas of brown wash peeping through but it should be fairly unobtrusive.

11 Rule a line around the firescreen 1cm (⅜in) from the edge. Where the firescreen is scalloped or curved, work freehand with the pencil. Paint over the line you have drawn, using a No. 4 brush dipped into slightly watered-down green paint. When you have gone all the way around the screen, add leaves on both sides of the line at regular intervals, using the tip of your brush. All the leaves point outwards (changing direction at the centre of the middle panel).

12 With the No. 6 brush, add gold paint to any appropriate edges. Add a red cross to your flag, using a No. 4 brush. When everything is dry, brush on a coat of antiquing liquid, removing the excess with a soft cloth. When dry, apply a coat of satin varnish to protect your artwork.

TEDDY BEAR TOY CHEST

TOY CHESTS ARE ALWAYS satisfying projects to undertake as there is lots of scope for colour and pattern and it is an excuse to use some of the more traditional nursery motifs, in this instance teddy bears.

This wooden box is of fairly simple construction but has nice set-in panels on all four sides, which means the design has a natural frame. I wanted something busy and colourful and so I painted the teddies in different colours, which also gave them individual personalities. You can explore this further by adding waistcoats or coloured bows. Or, if you want a less busy effect, you could paint the teddies on a plain background. Don't forget to choose a coordinating colour for the inside of the box. You could also paint a single teddy inside the lid – yet another incentive for

These teddies look quite at home leaning up against the teddy bear toy chest. You could use a child's favourite teddy as the model for the motifs on the toy chest you paint.

children to put their toys into the chest themselves.

If you have an old toy box that you want to transform, you could adapt this project to it, using a base coat of oil-based paint. If the panels are not set in, you could draw borders using a ruler to create a similar effect. The end result will certainly be something that will brighten a child's bedroom – or possibly even serve as an attractive storage box to hide away toys in another part of the house, such as the playroom or kitchen.

YOU WILL NEED

✪ *Toy chest in white, untreated wood*
✪ *Water-based paints in red, green and white (for base coats)*
✪ *2.5cm (1in) flat brush*
✪ *Nos. 4 and 6 artist's brushes (see Tip)*
✪ *Square stencil, approximately 3 x 3cm (1¼ x 1¼ in)*
✪ *Repositionable spray glue*
✪ *Stencil brush*
✪ *Water-based paints in black, medium brown, white, yellow, beige, dark brown and red (for decoration)*
✪ *Teddy stencil (see pages 90–1)*
✪ *Daisy stencil (see pages 122–5)*
✪ *Varnish and varnishing brush*

1 Using red paint and the flat brush, paint the two horizontal rails on each of the four sides, and the four rails on the lid, doing this as carefully as possible. Apply a second coat of red when the first is dry.

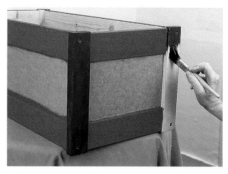

2 With the flat brush, paint the four uprights at the ends of the box green, using the No. 4 brush for the areas where the red and green paints meet. When dry, apply a second coat.

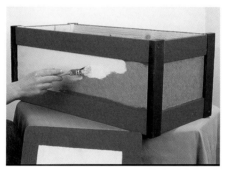

3 When the red and green coats are dry, fill in the central panels on all four sides and the lid with at least two coats of white paint, again using the flat brush and allowing it to dry between coats. When dry, check that the edges are neat, and do any touching up with the No. 6 brush.

4 Spray the back of the square stencil with glue and position at the centre of one white panel. Stencil it in black, applying the paint sparingly. Lift off the stencil and move it diagonally up or down to the next position. Repeat the process until you have filled each white panel with a chequerboard pattern. Don't worry about awkward spots around the edges that cannot be stencilled, as they are dealt with in the next step.

5 Using the No. 4 artist's brush and slightly watered-down black paint, fill in any gaps in the pattern that were too close to the edge to be stencilled.

6 When the paint is dry, spray the back of the teddy stencil with glue, and stencil a line of teddies on each of the chequerboard panels. Use medium brown for some of the teddies and white for others, planning the colour scheme in advance.

7 Dip the slightly stiff No. 6 brush into yellow and medium brown paint, and dab it on one of the brown teddies. You will see a rather pleasing textured effect emerge which passes as fur. Continue in this way over all the brown teddies, then do the same for the white teddies, using white and a little beige. (For more close-up detail on this, refer to the illustration on pages 90–1.)

8 When the teddies are dry, the details can be added using a No. 4 brush. For soft-looking fur, paint around the outline with tiny diagonal lines (see pages 90–1), using dark brown for the brown teddies and watered-down black for the white teddies. To create ears and also pads for the paws, use dark brown for the brown teddies and red for the white teddies. Give them all black eyebrows, plus small yellow discs for the eyes. When dry, paint in a black centre and a fine black line around each eye.

TIP **The No. 6 artist's brush needs to be an old one, on which the bristles have gone a little stiff. Failing that, you may just have to ruin a good brush! One way of doing this is by washing it badly and then leaving it on a radiator to dry.**

9 Use watered-down black paint and a No. 4 brush to shade the teddies, blending it in with your finger. With white paint and a No. 4 brush, highlight the curves on the brown teddies and the paw pads on the white teddies, again blending with your finger. Add a white dot on the pupil of each eye to add sparkle to the teddies' expressions.

10 Spray the back of the daisy stencil with glue and position it on the border. Stencil white daisies around the red and green borders of the box and lid. Remove the stencil. Fill in with white paint and a No. 4 brush. When the daisies are dry, fill in their centres with yellow and then shade lightly with watered-down black paint and a No. 4 brush (blending with your finger), to give the flowers dimension. Highlight the yellow centres with white using the same brush and, once again, your finger. To protect your handiwork from sticky fingers, varnish the chest.

DELFT TILE PATTERN CUSHIONS

Hand-painting creates an attractive, textured effect on this fabric. The single colour can be made to look surprisingly varied through the addition of a little water to the paint, creating a 'wash' effect.

THERE ARE MANY FABRIC PAINTS on the market which require a minimum amount of preparation to ensure that the paint stays where you put it. Remember to follow the instructions on the paint to avoid any disasters.

To work with, fabric is completely different from wood, ceramics or other hard surfaces. It is well worth trying, even if you start with an inexpensive snippet of calico. From my own point of view, the main drawback of working on fabric is that at some point I might be forced to sew! I have therefore made the next project as simple as possible for both artist and seamstress. The painted fabric I have made for this project uses just one colour: indigo blue (but any navy blue will do). When the painting was completed, I cut off the excess fabric, leaving about 1.5cm (⁵⁄₈in) all around. I turned this under using a hot iron and then sewed the painted panel onto an existing, larger cushion cover, which gave it a coloured border. There are all sorts of variations on this rather basic method that you could undertake according to your skills. You could, for example, use this piece for the front of a new cushion cover without a border, using the 1.5cm (⁵⁄₈in) excess fabric all around for seam allowances.

One final tip before you embark on this project is that you should draw your tile pattern onto paper first. This forward planning will enable you to overcome any problems with the pattern and design before you are wielding a paintbrush over a piece of fabric. Refer to the illustration on page 96 but feel free to incorporate other motifs that lend themselves to the style. They can be as simple or complex as you like.

YOU WILL NEED

- ✪ *White or light-coloured pure cotton fabric, at least 33 x 33cm (13¼in x 13¼in) and preferably larger*
- ✪ *Masking tape*
- ✪ *Piece of cardboard slightly smaller than the fabric*
- ✪ *Pencil*
- ✪ *Ruler*
- ✪ *No. 4 artist's brush*
- ✪ *Indigo (or navy blue) fabric paint*
- ✪ *Eraser*
- ✪ *Cushion*

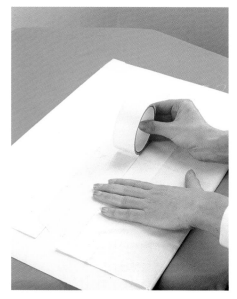

1 Iron the fabric thoroughly and then tape your piece of fabric to the piece of cardboard. This stretches out the fabric slightly to make it taut and gives a rigid, flat surface on which to paint.

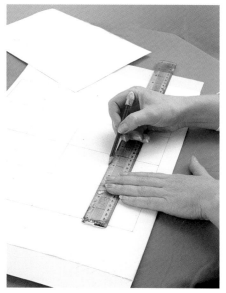

2 Using a pencil and ruler, lightly mark in the middle of the fabric a square measuring 30 x 30cm (12 x 12in). Divide it into quarters and then into sixteenths. You should have marked out 16 squares, each measuring 7.5 x 7.5cm (3 x 3in). Don't be concerned if your measurements are a few millimetres out.

TIP **Try a test patch of the fabric paint on your chosen fabric and then wash the fabric to make sure that the paint and fabric are completely compatible.**

3 Lightly pencil your tile patterns into each small square, either using the illustrations or templates traced from them as a guide, or copying your own practice sketches. Using the artist's brush and slightly watered-down indigo blue paint, go over the lines you have sketched. It is worthwhile doing some test strokes on the excess fabric around the edge as this will give you a feel for painting on something with a texture you are unused to and will make you more confident with your actual patterns.

TIP **When marking the fabric, use only a light pencil line – although the pencil marks can be erased, slight smudge marks are a risk.**

4 Carefully rub out any pencil lines that are still evident. Continue working on the pattern until you have filled in all the squares to your satisfaction. When you are quite happy with your fabric and it is completely dry, remove it carefully from the piece of cardboard. Iron it following the paint manufacturer's instructions, and mount it onto your chosen cushion.

GINGER JAR WALL PLAQUES

THERE IS A CLASSIC timelessness to these ginger jar motifs which will make them fit in with most themes and settings throughout the home. Their versatile design uses only three paint colours, so once you have the basic jar shape it is easy to customize the plaques to suit your own style and environment. Look around you – even your teacup might hold a simple pattern or motif that you can use to adorn one of the jars!

These auriculas were the first wall plaques I did, and they continue to give pleasure.

Making the paper templates for the ginger jars is a simple process, and you will probably find that when you are trimming them with scissors you invent your own shapes. As well as altering the shape or pattern of the jars, another way of personalizing this project would be to choose an alternative background colour.

The wooden plaques in the project are simply pieces of pine, which are easy to paint on. They can be obtained from any good timber merchant or DIY store, where they can be cut to the size you require. Ensure that the wood you choose doesn't have a very rough finish, as you will find it difficult to paint. On the other hand, some grain and visible knots are desirable, as they will add character to your work. This set of pine plaques makes a substantial and interesting picture group without the added costs of framing. The plaques look good either hung on a wall or displayed on a shelf, table or other surface.

YOU WILL NEED

✪ *4 pieces of pine, each about 23 x 23cm (9 x 9in)*
✪ *Fine-grade sandpaper*
✪ *Clean cloth*
✪ *2.5cm (1in) flat brush*
✪ *Water-based paints in white, beige, indigo and black*
✪ *4 ginger jar templates (see opposite)*
✪ *Pencil*
✪ *Repositionable spray glue*
✪ *Nos. 1, 4 and 8 artist's brushes*
✪ *Eraser*
✪ *Ruler*

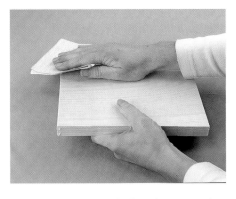

1 Sand the front and edge of your wooden plaque using fine-grade sandpaper to remove any splinters or rough areas, then dust it down with a damp cloth.

2 Using the flat brush, apply a coat of the white paint to the front and sides. Before this coat has dried, blend a light coat of beige carefully into the white paint. This adds a little depth and interest to the background and also helps the white jars stand out from it when finished.

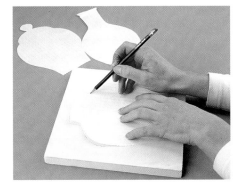

3 Position one of the ginger jar templates centrally on a piece of wood and then draw around it. To keep it still while you do this, you could use a little spray glue.

4 Remove the ginger jar template and fill in the jar shape using a No. 8 brush and white paint.

TIP **Spend a little time cutting different templates. You will find it rewarding and will eventually cut out the perfect pot shapes for your piece of wood.**

5 You are now ready to start decorating the jar. Lightly pencil in the pattern – try to do this freehand, as it will look more realistic. Experiment a little, as you can always erase it and try again. Begin by drawing lines which curve slightly across the jar. Fill in this grid with your motif.

6 When you are happy with the design, paint over the pencil lines with watered-down indigo paint, using a No. 1 brush. Now paint the motifs using the same brush and the same watered-down paint.

COCKEREL
TERRACOTTA
POTS

THIS TRIO OF JAUNTY cockerel motifs will add colour to a country kitchen or a more contemporary setting. The terracotta pots I have chosen as a base for the motifs are inexpensive and widely available from garden centres and DIY stores. You will find them easy to paint, as the porous surface of the terracotta takes the paint well and dries quickly.

These pots have been decorated with simple but colourful abstract designs. Use as many patterns as you can think of to create a bright and vibrant collection of pots.

I have used three styles of cockerel on the pots. To paint the black one, follow the steps supplied. For the white cockerel, follow the instructions for the black bird, substituting white for black. To paint the handsome coloured cockerel, use dark green for the main body and highlight the tail with a little yellow. When that is dry, paint the wing in terracotta and the neck and head in yellow, then follow the instructions for the black cockerel.

The dramatic results would make a lovely gift, especially filled with fresh herbs. As a final touch why not paint the name of the contents of each pot in an appropriate place? Either way, the trio will look bright and colourful displayed on any window-sill, shelf or surface around the home.

When you are confident with your cockerel motif, you could start to build up a collection of cockerel pots. There are lots of ways of making variations, either by altering background colours or simply by using terracotta pots of different sizes and styles.

YOU WILL NEED

- ✪ *Three terracotta pots, each about 12cm (5in) high*
- ✪ *Clean cloth*
- ✪ *Water-based paints in apple green, black, red, yellow, white, terracotta and dark green (for all 3 cockerels)*
- ✪ *2.5cm (1in) flat brush*
- ✪ *Cockerel stencil (see opposite)*
- ✪ *Repositionable spray glue*
- ✪ *Stencil brush*
- ✪ *Nos. 1, 4 and 6 artist's brushes*
- ✪ *Pencil*
- ✪ *Eraser*
- ✪ *Chalk (optional)*
- ✪ *Gold paint*
- ✪ *Varnish and varnishing brush*

TIP **When you are stencilling the cockerel onto the pot, it may feel slightly awkward to work on a curved surface, but if you hold the stencil firmly in place with one hand you can apply the paint with the other.**

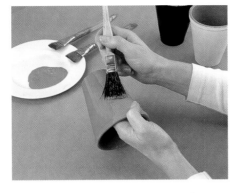

1 Carefully dust down your pot and remove any sticky labels. Apply the base coat of apple green to the outside using the flat brush. Only one coat will be needed and it should dry in a few minutes.

2 Spray the back of the cockerel stencil lightly with the glue and then position it on the pot. Stencil the cockerel in black using the stencil brush and then remove the stencil.

3 When dry, use a No. 6 brush to paint over the stencilled area with another coat of black. Depending on the opacity of your paints, you may need to apply a further coat to this when dry.

4 Use a sharp pencil to sketch in the crown and legs of the cockerel. Do this freehand – you can always erase and try again if you are not entirely happy with the proportions you have drawn.

The plain background is a perfect vehicle for these different-coloured auriculas.

5 Using a No. 4 brush, fill in the cockerel's crown and face with red paint. Again, you may need to apply two coats to achieve a bright red colour.

6 When dry, use the No. 4 brush to paint the beak, eye and legs in yellow paint. If you prefer, you can pencil or chalk them in first to get the proportions right. Add a second coat of yellow paint once the first has dried. Leave to dry.

7 Paint the detail with a No. 1 brush. With black paint, fill in the centre of the eye and apply a fine line around the edge. Add appropriate markings on the beak and some 'wrinkles' on the face as shown. The legs will need some black marks and lines to separate the toes. Dot the eye with white. Use watered-down white paint to outline the wing shape and feathering as a contrast to the black.

8 Shade the cockerel's legs and face with watered-down black paint, using a No. 4 brush and then blending it in with your finger. Highlight the face, wing, neck and tail with white paint applied with a No. 4 brush and then smudged with your finger.

The 16 compartment cubby-hole that accommodates these cockerel terracotta pots was probably once a letter rack in a hotel or institution of some kind. It is certainly a perfect way to show off this collection. I used six different background colours and varied the cockerels slightly to make each one individual but still part of the set.

9 As a finishing touch apply gold paint to the rim of the pot, using a No. 4 brush. When it is dry you can consider further embellishment, such as evenly spaced coloured dots in contrasting colours around the gold rim. When dry, varnish.

GARDEN

DECORATED BIRDHOUSES

COLLECTIONS OF BIRDHOUSES, either painted or unpainted, look lovely in the garden. I find them an irresistible buy and enjoy painting them to complement my existing collection. They seem to be available now from many garden centres, mail order catalogues and craft shops. I try to keep my painting themes for them sympathetic to the garden surroundings but have found that it is nice to create a splash of colour among the greenery.

The shape of this birdhouse lent itself to decoration with two tall topiary trees as well as small birds. With the painted pots beneath the trees, this design brought in considerably more colour and detail. If you want to add more colour still, add some fruit to the trees or a flower border.

While I have used mainly bird and garden motifs for these birdhouses, there are, of course, many alternative design possibilities. One possible theme would be a selection of oriental birdhouses using some of the patterns from the Miniature Oriental Chest (page 72). Alternatively, Delft tile-patterned birdhouses, based on the designs for the cushions (page 94), could look extremely smart. Because the birdhouses work well as sets, you could plan the designs so that each is a different variation on a particular theme. Make the decoration as fun and whimsical as you like – the sky is literally the limit when it comes to these garden furnishings!

If you plan to leave your birdhouses outside all year round, it would be prudent to weatherproof them first. Prime the bare wood with an acrylic primer before applying the base coats and the decoration, and then finish with a coat or two of polyurethane varnish.

YOU WILL NEED

✪ *Birdhouse, either painted or unpainted*
✪ *Water-based paint for base colour (if birdhouse is unpainted)*
✪ *2.5cm (1in) flat brush (if birdhouse is unpainted)*
✪ *Chalk or pencil*
✪ *Water-based paints in white, yellow, black and light green*
✪ *Nos. 1 and 4 artist's brushes*

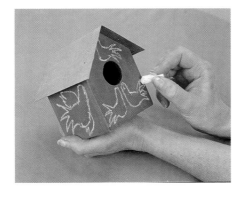

1 My birdhouse came with the base colour already painted. If yours is unpainted, then simply apply your chosen base colour using the flat brush. When dry, draw a simple design on it with chalk or pencil.

2 Fill in each of your birds with white paint, using the No. 4 brush. When they are dry, build up the colour with a second coat. Leave to dry.

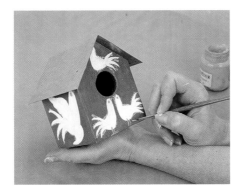

3 Using a No. 1 brush, add yellow eyes and beaks to all the birds, and legs to those birds that are not in flight.

4 When dry, use slightly watered-down black paint on the No.1 brush to add details to each bird. These include a thin line outlining the shape; feather details on the wings and tail; lines on the legs, feet and beak; and the centre of the eye.

TIP **If you are not confident about drawing your designs freehand, then make small stencils instead.**

5 Lightly shade the birds with watered-down black paint using the No. 4 brush. Dot their eyes with white, using the No. 1 brush. Using chalk or pencil, draw in a line on which you can paint a garland of leaves. I have done this around the entrance hole on the front, and the bird at the side of the box is trailing a spray of leaves. With light green paint and the No. 4 brush, paint over the pencil line and then paint in the leaves.

COLOURWASHED GARDEN BENCH & TABLE

G ARDEN FURNITURE IS becoming more and more widely available in an 'unfinished' state, giving you scope for choosing your own colour of wood stain or paint. In the case of this bench and table, I wanted to produce a nice, light effect, suitable for summertime. As they would be outdoors for a good part of the year, they had to be prepared and finished in a weather-resistant medium. For the base coat I used an acrylic wood primer, which I worked into all the nooks and crannies to protect the pieces from the elements. Two coats of polyurethane varnish will give extra protection.

YOU WILL NEED

✪ Garden bench and table in untreated white wood
✪ Acrylic wood primer in white
✪ 5cm (2in) flat brush
✪ Medium-grade sandpaper
✪ Clean cloth
✪ Acrylic scumble glaze or colourwash mix
✪ Water-based paint in turquoise to tint glaze
✪ Polyurethane varnish and varnishing brush

1 First the garden bench and table need to be thoroughly painted with acrylic wood primer, using the flat brush. Start by turning them upside down and painting the undersides. Work the brush in between the slats and try to cover every bit of exposed wood with the primer. Turn them right side up again and paint the rest.

2 When the bench and table are completely dry, rub them down with a medium-grade sandpaper. You will find that some areas are quite rough, and sanding will make the wash much easier to apply, as well as becoming a much more comfortable piece of furniture. Pay particular attention to sanding the backrest, seat and arms. Wipe the surface down with a damp cloth to remove dust.

3 Mix the colourwash to the desired depth of colour, and apply it using the flat brush. If you wish to test the colour first, then paint it on the underside of one of the pieces. Remember that two light layers of wash are always more effective than one heavy one. When dry, add a second layer of wash. Leave overnight to dry and then apply two coats of varnish, allowing it to dry between coats.

BLUE & WHITE GARDEN SLABS

THESE SLABS WOULD BE a cheap and original way of adding some colour and pattern to a patio area. Made from precast concrete, they were remarkably inexpensive. What is more, they could easily be customized to suit the surroundings. If you wanted a more Mediterranean look, for example, you could simply incorporate some terracotta paint. I am afraid I

The blue and white combination makes an eye-catching feature in a garden setting.

can't make any promises on their longevity, as they are a new venture for me and I have not had the time to put them through the four-seasons test. However, with their polyurethane coatings, they ought – in theory – to last a considerable time. Even now, they are out in the rain on a cold winter's day and not showing any signs of fatigue!

I have given step-by-step instructions for painting one of the designs but by referring to the artwork on page 120 you will be able to use all four. Or, for an alternative design, you could adapt the motifs on page 96. When finished, they can be set into grass or gravel or within an existing patio. On a nice warm summer's day, there is no reason why you shouldn't paint existing slabs in situ, although you would need to clean them well first.

I painted these slabs in mid-winter, and as they had been outside when I bought them, they were rather damp. I found that by leaning them up against a warm radiator they dried out well. They also retained a lot of heat, which made them positively cosy to paint. One word of warning. These slabs are *very* heavy so do take care when lifting them – be careful of your back, and *don't* drop them on your toes.

YOU WILL NEED

✪ *4 precast concrete slabs*

✪ *Emulsion paint in magnolia (for base coat)*

✪ *2.5cm (1in) flat brush*

✪ *Ruler*

✪ *Pencil*

✪ *Water-based paint in dark blue (for decoration)*

✪ *Nos. 4 and 6 artist's brushes*

✪ *Antiquing liquid and varnishing brush*

✪ *Polyurethane varnish*

1 Paint each slab with magnolia emulsion using the flat brush, and when dry apply a second coat. Leave to dry.

2 Using a ruler and pencil, mark out a grid of squares on the slab. If you want to be precise, you can measure first, but I find that by just using your 'eye' you can achieve a more rustic effect.

TIP **Before varnishing the slabs with polyurethane, I applied antiquing liquid to stop them from looking too new.**

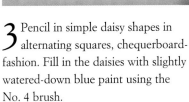

3 Pencil in simple daisy shapes in alternating squares, chequerboard-fashion. Fill in the daisies with slightly watered-down blue paint using the No. 4 brush.

4 Still using the No. 4 brush and watered-down blue paint, carefully follow the vertical and horizontal pencil lines of the original grid you created. Fill in the squares that don't have daisies with this, too, using the No. 6 brush. When dry, apply antiquing liquid with a varnishing brush, wiping off any excess with a soft cloth. Then, when that is dry, use the same brush to paint on a coat of varnish for extra protection outside.

TEMPLATES

BIRD IN A TREE
Bird in a Tree Wall Pattern
P26

HERALDIC SHIELD
Coat of Arms Mural
P28

DIAMOND
Coat of Arms Mural &
Harlequin Wall
P28 & 24

FLEUR-DE-LIS
Coat of Arms Mural
P28

MALTESE CROSS
Coat of Arms Mural
P28

LION
Coat of Arms Mural
P28

DAISY
Elephant Motif Bed, Teddy Bear
Toy Chest & Country Castle
Mural
P64, 88 & 38

STAR
Country Castle Mural
P38

CASTLE TOWER
Coat of Arms Mural & Country Castle Mural
P28 & 38

BIRD
Coat of Arms Mural &
Country Castle Mural
P28 & 38

TASSEL
Oriental Trompe l'Oeil Rug
P32

ORIENTAL STENCIL
Oriental Trompe l'Oeil Rug & Pineapple Bedside Cabinet
P32 & 58

BIRDHOUSE I
Tree and Birdhouse Firescreen
P82

BIRDHOUSE II
Tree and Birdhouse Firescreen
P82

RESOURCES

Belinda Ballantine
The Old Bear House
53 High Street
Malmesbury
Wiltshire SN16 9AG
Tel: 01666 841144
(Decorative painting supplies
and white wooden items)

Dulux Paints
ICI Paints
Wexham Road, Slough
Berkshire SL2 5DS
Tel: 01753 550000 (Contact
for your nearest stockist)

Fired Earth
117–119 Fulham Road
London SW3 6R4
Tel: 0171 589 0489
(Range of own brand paints
available in sample pots)

Green & Stone
259 King's Road
London SW3 5ER
Tel: 0171 352 0837
(Paints, artist's and stencilling materials, specialist
brushes)

Habitat
Tel: 0171 255 2545 (Contact
for your nearest branch – own
range of paints and items
to paint)

Harvey Baker Designs Ltd.
Unit 1
Rodgers Industrial Estate
Yalberton Road
Paignton
Devon TQ4 7PJ
Tel: 01803 521515 (Wide
range of MDF blanks for
painting or découpage)

Hobbycraft
Tel: 01202 596100 (Contact
for your nearest branch –
chain of craft supply stores
with a wide range of items
for decorative painting)

IKEA
Tel: 0181 208 5600 (Contact
for your nearest branch –
wide range of items to paint)

Laura Ashley
Tel: 01686 622116 (Contact
for your nearest branch –
range of own brand paints
available in sample pots)

Liberon Waxes Ltd.
Mountfield Industrial Estate
Learoyd Road
New Romney
Kent TN28 8XU
Tel: 01797 367555
(Wide range of gilt varnishes
in metallic colours)

London Graphic Centre
107–115 Long Acre
London WC2E 9N2
Tel: 0171 240 0095
(Fabric paints)

Old Village Paint Store
Heart of the Country
Swinfen
Nr. Lichfield
Staffordshire WS14 9QR
Tel: 01543 480669
(Everything you ever wanted
for decorative painting:
a wide range of paints,
varnishes, colourwashes,
craft paints, stencils,
brushes, MDF blanks and
helpful advice)

Paper & Paints
4 Park Walk
London SW10 OAD
Tel: 0171 352 8676
(A large range of specialist
paints, brushes, pigments
and varnishes)

The Tales Press
Dam Street
Lichfield
Staffordshire
Tel: 01543 256777
(Paints, artist's materials,
brushes and stencilling
materials)